146

LITURGY AND SOCIAL JUSTICE

Celebrating Rites—Proclaiming Rights

Three Papers and Two Homilies Given at the 1988
National Meeting of the Federation of Diocesan
Liturgical Commissions

Papers
Dianne Bergant, C.S.A.
Thea Bowman, F.S.P.A.
J. Bryan Hehir

Homilies
Raymond G. Hunthausen
James Lopresti, S.J.

Editor: Edward M. Grosz

THE LITURGICAL PRESS
Collegeville, Minnesota

Cover design by MARY JO PAULY

9	8	7	6	5	4	3	2	1

Library of Congress Catalog Card Number: 89-63328

Contents

Foreword

God invites everyone to the Eucharistic table, where all can feast and be challenged, nourished, and refreshed as a pilgrim people. To the liturgy come all those who were the special concern of the Christus in his ministry of outreach: the poor, the oppressed, the minorities, those misunderstood and cast aside by society.

As Archbishop Hunthausen remarks in the homily for the opening session, "The liturgy is a mirror, an image of what the kingdom is like." During the liturgy we set aside all titles, ranks, privileges, and categories. Within the context of liturgy all God's people hear the Word of God, a Word challenging believers to see who they are and who they must become as ministers of peace and reconciliation. All are called to that evangelical ministry, a ministry that implies an ongoing death, a death to all that is contrary to the values of the gospel kingdom. In that experience of death a new people and a new world are reborn.

To worship "in sincerity and in truth" is to be deeply rooted in the cost of discipleship: to pay the price in service of the poor, the needy, and those broken in body, mind, heart, and spirit. To worship in sincerity and truth is to open one's ears and heart to the cries of the poor. To worship in sincerity and in truth is to acknowledge that racism, sexism, militarism, the arms race, poverty, hatred, and oppression of every sort have no place in the proclamation of the "good news" of the kingdom.

In the final analysis, worship moves our communities to work for a just social order, as it schools all sincere disciples of the Lord in the truth of the gospel values of the kingdom to become ambassadors of peace and workers for social reform, wherever there is injustice in the world.

The liturgy provides us with a vision of the possibilities the kingdom offers us and those whose lives we touch, as we get up enough nerve to begin changing the way things are in our social and cultural structures, our politics and economics, our cities, streets, and neighborhoods.

As we accept the invitation to come to the table of the Lord, our response to that invitation must lead us to be serious about our commitment to "do justice" for the sake of the kingdom: that the blind may see, the deaf hear, the lame walk, the dead be raised to life, and the poor have the gospel preached to them (Matthew 11:2-6).

MONSIGNOR EDWARD M. GROSZ, DIRECTOR
OFFICE OF WORSHIP
DIOCESE OF BUFFALO, NEW YORK

Homily for the Opening Session

RAYMOND G. HUNTHAUSEN

> "Rolling up the scroll, he handed it back to the attendant and sat down, and the eyes of all in the synagogue looked intently at him. He said to them, 'Today this scripture passage is fulfilled in your hearing.' And all spoke highly of him and were amazed at the gracious words that came from his mouth" (Luke 4:20-21).

Jesus has stood up in the synagogue, in the place of worship, and announced that Isaiah's words are being fulfilled as they listen, and that the kingdom or reign of God is here. He is preaching the kingdom, even illustrating the kingdom, within a liturgical setting. Liturgy and the reign of God are intimately related. It is impossible to worship God in good conscience and ignore our clear responsibilities to work at building up that kingdom. In fact, as the recovery of our scriptural and liturgical tradition suggests, the liturgy becomes a kind of measuring stick, to show us how our culture and our society measure up to the standards of God's kingdom. Liturgy is not unlike a parable, not so much teaching us something, but provoking and challenging us—even daring us—to resist the status quo and to sharpen our vision of the kingdom.

There are exciting possibilities today as we begin to recover this sense of liturgy as a mirror, an image, of what the kingdom is like. It is God who extends the invitation to as-

7

semble, and all are welcome. All people, and especially the oppressed, are greeted and embraced. All people, and especially God's poor, hear the good news preached to them. When we enter the liturgy we set aside all our usual categories and titles and ranks and privileges. The only distinctions we need are those based on initiation and ministry. Otherwise, *all* are sprinkled, *all* are incensed, *all* are blessed, *all* are invited to the Lord's banquet table. This is indeed what the reign of God is like.

In December 1987 the Holy Father issued an encyclical called "On Social Concerns," and many of the points he makes deserve constant repetition. While he offers us a hopeful vision of the future, he is likewise clear that God's justice is far from realized today. He says that "this present period of time, on the eve of the third Christian millenium, is characterized by a widespread expectancy, rather like a new 'Advent,' which to some extent touches everyone"(4). In the meantime, he insists, we cannot close our eyes to what is around us. He says that "preference for the poor" has to "embrace the immense multitudes of the hungry, the needy, the homeless, those without medical care and, above all, those without hope of a better future. It is impossible not to take account of the existence of these realities. To ignore them would mean becoming like the 'rich man' who pretended not to know the beggar Lazarus lying at his gate"(42).

Pope John Paul insists that there is a sense of immediacy about this task of kingdom-building. "There is no justification," he says, "for despair or pessimism or inertia . . . . I wish to appeal with simplicity and humility to everyone, to all men and women without exception. I wish to ask them to be convinced of the seriousness of the present moment and of each one's individual responsibility, and to implement, by the use of their resources, by their civic activity, by contributing to economic and political decisions, and by personal commitment to national and international undertakings, the measures inspired by solidarity and love of preference for the poor. This is what is demanded by the present moment and above all by the very dignity of the human person, the indestructible image of God the creator, which is identical in each one of us.

"In this commitment, the sons and daughters of the Church must serve as examples and guides, for they are called upon, in conformity with the program announced by Jesus himself, in the synagogue at Nazareth, to 'preach good news to the poor . . . to proclaim release to the captives and recovery of sight to the blind, to set at liberty those who are oppressed, to proclaim the acceptable year of the Lord' "(47).

The Holy Father then goes on to connect this challenging vision of God's justice to liturgical celebration. He says, "Here on earth the kingdom of God is already present in mystery. The kingdom becomes present above all in the celebration of the sacrament of the Eucharist . . . . All of those who partake in the Eucharist are called to discover, through this sacrament, the profound meaning of our actions in the world in favor of development and peace, and to receive from it the strength to commit ourselves ever more generously, following the example of Christ, who in this sacrament lays down his life for his friends" (48).

I would share these final thoughts with you today on how difficult it sometimes is to help build up the kingdom; some thoughts on the cost of discipleship; what liturgy is all about; what Sunday is all about; what the paschal mystery is; some thoughts on life overcoming death by God's power.

But first there must be death, and there are so many kinds of death. People sat in awe before Jesus as he stood in the synagogue and told them about the kingdom, and how Isaiah's vision of the future was actually taking shape right now. But later in the day, as Jesus began to explain some of the demands of discipleship, some of the conversion required of kingdom-seekers, Luke explains that these hometown people "were all filled with fury. They rose up, drove him out of town, and led him to the brow of the hill on which their town had been built, to hurl him down headlong."

How often our own ministry of kingdom-building, of comparing the status quo with the possibilities the reign of God offers us, puts us somewhere between being run out of town and being led to the brow of the hill to be cast over the edge. The only hope in all of this, a hope most fully expressed and made present at liturgy, is the promise of Jesus that giving one's self fully for others means a passage from death to life—that death is indeed overcome, as well as anything that has to do with death: racisim, sexism, militarism, the arms race, sickness, poverty, hatred, oppression of every sort.

This is a magnificent vision, a vision that the liturgy constantly puts before us. During the liturgy we have a glimpse of what the kingdom could be like. While there, we can compare the status quo with the possibilities the kingdom offers us, and we can get up enough nerve to begin changing the way things are in our social and cultural structures, in our politics and economics, in our cities, our streets, and in our neighborhoods. Liturgy can free us from what the Holy Father calls our inertia, because liturgy shows us, if even for an hour, what the possibilities are. The liturgy offers us that vision today, as it did in the synagogue at Nazareth, when Jesus stood up to do the reading. They all had their eyes fixed on him, not because he was Jesus, not because he had grown up in their town, but because he was assuring them that what they had hoped and longed for was actually beginning to happen. He speaks those same words of promise and assurance to us now:

" 'Today this scripture passage is fulfilled in your hearing.' And all spoke highly of him and were amazed at the gracious words that came from his mouth."

Liturgy and Scripture: Creating a New World

DIANNE BERGANT, C.S.A.

This address takes as its starting point a statement from Mark Searle's book *Liturgy and Social Justice* (The Liturgical Press, 1980): "Like the word of God in history, the liturgy is the revelation of God's justice in both event and word. . . ." This presentation is an attempt to show my fundamental agreement with that statement. Before I begin, I would like to make a few preliminary remarks which will set the framework for my argument. I make these remarks as a biblical theologian, not as an expert in liturgy. However, as a member of a worshiping community, I have participated in celebrations of word and sacrament for quite a few years, and I have done extensive reflection on the meaning of worship and the role played by the biblical tradition within it.

First, I agree with those liturgical theologians who claim that justice is constitutive of worship. I am convinced that we must do more than simply make use of justice themes within liturgical celebrations. Secondly, I understand biblical interpretation as moving beyond a mere retrieval of the original meaning intended by the author. Because of the polyvalent (or multiple meanings) nature of a metaphor such as "exodus" or "reign of God" or "God's justice" (metaphors that I will discuss in this address), I believe that rich possibilities of interpretation call us forward with new insights and new meanings into new worlds. Thirdly, I maintain that both liturgy and biblical interpretation, in distinct yet complementary ways, function to create that new world called "the reign of God." Let me explain each point.

JUSTICE AS CONSTITUTIVE OF WORSHIP

The relationship between liturgy and social justice has been the focus of attention of many people within the recent past. In an effort to awaken within the community a sense of social responsibility, those who prepare liturgies often choose prayers and biblical readings that do more than merely soothe the spirits of the assembly or pay tribute to its accomplishments. Acknowledging that the liturgy is the primary source of spiritual nourishment for the majority of the congregation, they seek to provide there a diet that will not only assuage some vague feeling of emptiness but will also renew the very life of the worshiping body. Their goal is the conscientization of the entire believing community. There have been varying degrees of success in this venture. As often as people have been converted to social consciousness, others have been repelled by it. The extreme individualism chronicled by Robert Bellah *et al.* in *Habits of the Heart* (University of California Press, 1985) is deeply entrenched in contemporary society.

Liturgy is also important to many already awakened social ministers. They turn to worship in search of inspiration and courage and assistance. They see the liturgy as the font from which flows the power of God that will sustain and nourish them. They search for a worshiping community that shares their commitment and will support them in their efforts at social reform.

Without questioning the significance of such perceptions, one can legitimately espouse a more dynamic understanding of liturgy. According to such a view, liturgy not only proclaims and celebrates what has been accomplished but it also announces and anticipates what has not yet been fully realized. In a very real sense, liturgy is itself the very act of establishing the reign of God. It is a sacramental or symbolic act that creates the reality it signifies. It initiates a transformation that is intended to spread beyond the confines of the gathered assembly. In this sense, justice issues are more than merely themes introduced in prayers, songs, or readings during the ritual performance. Justice issues are constitutive of the liturgical act itself. The very makeup of the assembly and the manner in which the rite is performed reflect the degree to which justice is celebrated.

Social justice is rooted in another related but quite different concept, i.e., the justice of God. It is this latter justice that the liturgy celebrates. As is the case with every characterization of God, the notion of divine justice is better understood as a metaphor than as a definition. This is certainly the case in the biblical tradition, where what we call justice is usually referred to as righteousness.

There, righteousness is used in relation to a balance and harmony within society. It is the kind of balance that not only allows individuals to follow their own inner directions, but also fosters their growth, their flowering, and their full bloom. It does this while at the same time weighing the force of the individual against the vigor of each of the others within the group. Righteousness is an ineffable governing capacity, like the genius of the conductor that teases out the potential of each instrument, knowing when its tones should dominate and when they should support the melody. It is like the artistry of the painter, who brushes brilliance next to subtleties in such right proportion as to create a work of distinctive beauty.

Such righteousness or harmonious balance is beyond our ability to comprehend, for we cannot sound the depths of the human spirit wherein is found the real identity of the individual. We are ignorant of the dignity of which each one of us is capable, of the warmth and devotion, of the love. Such righteousness belongs to God, who alone searches the human heart and knows the secret longings found there, who alone can weave the warp and woof of the countless tones and textures of society into a fabric that features each at the expense of none. It is the righteousness of God that knows the appropriate time and measure of each one's entrance, that can subdue or silence without putting to death.

Because it is of God, this righteousness is both within us and beyond us. It is the ground upon which each human relationship stands. It is the standard against which all else is judged. And yet it cannot be scrutinized by us. Because it is of God, it is constant and true; it is enlivening and discerning; it is merciful and compassionate. It knows what is in our best interests far better than we ourselves know, but it does not impose itself upon us. It calls to us gently but constantly. It calls through the tension we feel between our own need to be seen and heard and the right that others have for the same expression. We feel it in the passion we experience when we see others dispossessed or neglected or abandoned. These are the promptings in our lives of the righteousness that is of God.

Our own attempts at justice are but faint reflections of this righteousness. As fleeting as these ever-recurring reflections may be, our vitality as a people is dependent upon our ability to live according to them. We cannot capture them once and for all, because righteousness is not a static reality. It is supple and responsive to the tendencies and variations of changing human beings, not like the laws and statutes that are intended to guard it. And righteousness is certainly much more than obedience to these same laws and statutes.

We cannot fully comprehend this righteousness, nor can we force it to meet our narrow and unyielding standards of justice. Still, we glimpse it every time we hold another with respect and care. We can long for it, we can search for it, we can try to live in accord with it, and we can fashion our worship after its ideals, halting though our attempts may be. To the extent that we realize this righteousness in our midst, we are establishing the reign of God. Since liturgy is a sacramental or symbolic act that creates this reign, the righteousness of God is at its very heart.

The notion that liturgy is creative as well as expressive is not a Vatican II innovation. In the early 1920s, the Norwegian biblical scholar Sigmund Mowinckel wrote his now famous work entitled *Psalmenstudien,* studies of the psalms of ancient Israel, wherein he outlined the relationship between worship and eschatology. In his investigation of the festival of the Enthronement of Yawheh, he claimed that the dramatization of the myth of creation was more than a reenactment of primordial events. Because the reality of the actual Israelite community fell short of its religious and political expectations, its hopes were transposed into a future time. The cultic drama thus functioned as an announcement of an alternative to the present world.

Although biblical critics with historical concerns have challenged several of Mowinckel's claims, his point regard-

ing the creative function of cult seems to resonate with contemporary liturgical thinking. It is also fundamental to the
biblical scholar Walter Brueggemann's examination of the
world-making function of the psalms in his book *Israel's
Praise* (Fortress Press, 1988).

BIBLICAL INTERPRETATION: CREATING NEW WORLDS

The recent shift from historical-critical to literary-critical
methods of biblical analysis has led many interpreters away
from a rigid understanding of interpretation as description
of the originally intended meaning to a more creative perception of it as a kind of redescription resulting in new meanings. No longer do scholars merely search for some kind of
objective meaning preserved from the past. They seek ways
of creating new meanings for the present which will lead
into a better future. They enter into dialogue with the biblical texts, realizing that as in every *real* conversation, each
dialogue partner contributes something unique to the exchange.

It was precisely out of such a dialogical dynamic that
the biblical tradition developed in the first place. A careful
study of the Bible will show that first the ancient Israelite
and then the early Christian communities constantly interpreted and reinterpreted older traditions. The ongoing development of the tradition did not consist merely in the
handing down of static formulations. It also included the re-
peated process of reinterpreting earlier material within new
contexts. (As I see it, this is precisely the role of biblical
preaching.) Changes in the political, social, or religious
worlds necessitated new expressions of fundamental faith
as well as the articulation of new insights. The interaction

between historical events and forces both within and impinging upon the community influenced the shape of the tradition.

This formative process might have continued to the present day had not significant events compelled the community to single out and endorse certain specific traditions and statements over others and to confer authority on them. The destruction of the Solomonic temple at the time of the Babylonian Exile (*ca.* 587–538 B.C.E.) was one such event. The destruction of the Herodian temple at the time of the emergence of early Christianity (*ca.* 70 C.E.) was a second historical watershed. The final judgment deciding the canonical content of the tradition (Council of Trent, 1546) was yet another. Those of us committed to biblical preaching must remember that the closing of the canon did not mean the cessation of this revelatory process. It simply meant that new interpretations would not be considered canonical.

An examination of the biblical theme "exodus" might demonstrate the world-making nature of biblical interpretation. This theme is chosen not because it lends itself to the argument of my presentation, but because it characterizes the founding event of ancient Israel; it is the fundamental theological symbol of Yahwistic religion, and it became equally significant in the early Christian attempt to understand the revelation of God in Jesus the Christ. In a very real sense, the "exodus" theme is constitutive to biblical interpretation.

The concept "exodus" can be understood in a number of ways. In the first place, it refers to the historical event or events which brought Israel as a people into existence. It designates historical revolt from either Egyptian imperialism or Canaanite city-state feudalism. It further connotes the rejection of the rigid sociopolitical structures of those worlds, structures which claimed to be divinely ordained and eternally valid. These claims made Israel's social revolt a religious rebellion as well. Israel replaced these oppressive socioreligious structures with a kind of inclusive confederation that enacted laws which governed tribal and intertribal relationships. These laws forbade anything that might lead to the subjection of one free Israelite to another. (It is important to acknowledge here that Israelite society was patriarchal in structure and androcentric in focus. Free Israelites were adult males.)

"Exodus" can also refer to a cluster of themes which constitute the theological meaning of this historical experience of social revolt and religious rebellion. Within these themes we see God revealed as (1) particularly concerned with the oppressed and the mistreated, (2) accompanying the people in their movements out of oppression, and (3) leading them into the future toward *shalom*. As a theological symbol, "exodus" served to remind Israel of its revolutionary beginnings and of its religious, social, and political responsibilities. Through the ages both Jewish and Christian communities have understood events in history and in individual lives in terms of this "exodus" symbol. In fact, it has become the primary paradigm for theologies of liberation.

Finally, "exodus" can serve as a model for interpreting any or all of history as well as the traditions and practices that flow from history. The elements of the theological symbol just described function as the basis of an interpretive approach. First, there is the prominent theme of God's concern for the oppressed and mistreated. This theme, which was given expression in covenant law, boldly points out that the basic emphasis of the tradition is inclusive, i.e., it is addressed to all the people without exception. To perceive this theme of inclusiveness as fundamental to the tradition is to suggest that the message of the text, the community from which the text arose, and the context of the interpreter must all be critiqued from this inclusive point of view. (Several prominent radical feminist theologians have recently alleged that the tradition is intrinsically patriarchal and androcentric, and therefore unredeemable. I am much more of a revisionist. I believe that the dynamic of the tradition is basically inclusive regardless of how, over the centuries, the community has interpreted it and used it to discriminate.)

Secondly, the conviction that God accompanies the people in their movements out of oppression locates revelation squarely in the realm of history, and a history that is not static. While historical-critical methods seek to discover the earliest testimonies to the self-revelation of God, a dynamic historical consciousness, as advocated here, can more readily lead to an appreciation of the new and fresh revelatory possibilities of the present moment. God did not cease to self-disclose once the content of the canon had been determined. We believe that God is dynamically and purposefully present in our midst, revealing and calling to us in the circumstances of our contemporary existence.

Finally, commitment to a God who leads the people forward toward *shalom* or fullness of being, redirects attention away from some distant irretrievable past and beyond any abstract philosophical approach with its static categories to the challenging possibilities of the future. Thus a healthy living tradition is not restricted or confined to particular past or even to present meanings. The future holds an as yet unexplored treasury of meaning. This more dynamic historical approach has been clearly argued by such interpretive theorists as Paul Ricoeur (*Interpretation Theory*, Texas Christian University Press, 1976) and David Tracy *(Analogical Imagination,* Crossroad, 1981). In summary, a comprehensive inclusive critique, a dynamic historical consciousness, and an openness to what theorists call a "surplus of meaning" constitute the basis of an interpretive approach rooted in the theme "exodus."

THE REIGN OF GOD

Both liturgical performance and reinterpretation of the biblical tradition are world-making. But this making of new worlds is due to the revelatory presence of God, not to the expertise of those human persons involved in either enterprise. This God who is revealed is the God of righteousness, as righteousness has been described here. It is the God who includes all and expects that all be included. Celebrating this God, proclaiming the saving word of this God, brings God's reign into a world not yet completely fashioned in God's image.

The reign of God is an alternative way of living in the world, a world that has played a very active role in forming us into the people we have become. We possess many of the features of that world (e.g., our political and economic values), and we carry the effects of its history (e.g., our inherited prejudices). The reign of God challenges our preconceived judgments, our unexamined values, and our uncritical perception of reality. It seeks to transform our world first of all by opening us to new possibilities, to another way of perceiving the world and of living within it.

We are not always aware of the ways in which our world-view promotes our own well-being and enhances our lives.

It is very easy to take for granted the attitudes and mores into which we have been socialized. Usually, it is only when we find ourselves in situations where we feel restricted or in some way diminished, that we begin to question the appropriateness, even the justice, first of the situation and then of its underlying presuppositions. This conscious process explains why those who suffer oppression or who are relegated to marginality or invisibility within a society are sometimes better critics of that society than are those who are privileged and satisfied. And what is more, this is true of ecclesial communities as well as social and political organizations. It is precisely in these areas that the inbreaking of the reign of God can transform our minds and hearts and offer us an alternative.

This alternative can operate on several different levels. It can sensitize us to language and imagery and gestures that explicitly insult, subtly minimize, or completely disregard any members of the community. It can alert us to situations in which individuals or groups are relegated to tasks that are always subordinate and exclusively auxiliary by nature. It can challenge presuppositions of an anthropology from which flow sexism, racism, classism, ageism, handicapism, nationalism, chauvinism of any kind.

As mentioned earlier, I believe that the dynamic of the biblical tradition is fundamentally inclusive. I also believe that, at its root, liturgy is inclusive as well. However, we must admit that neither the biblical tradition nor liturgical experience has a history free of discrimination. This inclusive dynamic, as well as the acknowledgment of our propensity to act out of preference, makes serious demands on us. Basically, the demands are these: the message of the biblical text, the community from which the text arose, the contemporary world in which we find ourselves, and the personal biases of the interpreter must all be critiqued by the values inherent in the reign of God. The same kind of critique is demanded with regard to the liturgy. Its structure, its movements, its cultural presuppositions, its imagery and language, its participatory character must stand humbly before the critical and transformative dynamic of God's reign.

The perplexing question that faces us here is not the degree to which the believing community willingly stands open before this transforming God, but its ability to recognize the demands of God's reign. Just what constitutes this alternative way of living in today's world? Before we can even begin to address that question, we must look briefly at the prevailing world-view or attitude toward life found in our Western culture.

By what criteria do we judge a person a success? What is the "pearl of great price" for which we seem willing to sacrifice all else in order to possess? For many, life is a series of challenges, and people are judged according to their ability to meet these challenges and to emerge triumphant. For others, the "pearl of great price" appears to be security, whether this is personal, economic, or national. All of these views reflect a hidden predilection toward mastery and control. We are intent on conquering, conquering the secrets of the universe, the forces of nature, or any competitor in the fields of sports, industry, politics, or international affairs. Once we have conquered, we devise elaborate systems for maintaining control lest we lose our positions of ascendancy. Having conquered and sustained sufficient control, we can then avail ourselves of whatever resources are at hand that might further our mastery.

These attitudes permeate our lives and influence all of

our relationships, whether with God, with each other, or with the rest of the natural world. As pervasive as these attitudes may be, if they are not tempered with other concerns, they can bring about in us a serious distortion of reality. It is precisely here that we must listen to those singular voices that have not been heard before, voices in the world and voices in the Church. Voices that call for collaboration rather than arbitrary control, for cooperation rather than competition, for interdependence rather than independence or dependence, for mutuality rather than domination or subjugation, for justice rather than exploitation, for respect rather than disdain, for compassion rather than indifference, for the reign of God rather than business as usual.

It is values such as these that must be brought into dialogue with both Scripture and liturgy. These are the kinds of ideals that must be enfleshed in the community. Such values and ideals offer us a challenging alternative way of living in our world. Let us not think, however, that this alternative way called for by the reign of God is a withdrawal from the real world. Quite the contrary. Even contemporary science and technology have brought us to realize that without attitudes of cooperation, interdependence, and mutuality, our very physical survival may be endangered, to say nothing of our political and international stability.

The challenge before us is a comprehensive one. However, there is no one of us who cannot incarnate some aspect of the just reign of God. We prepare liturgies and enlist people to participate. We choose biblical passages and select or compose communal prayers, and we use this liturgical language to forward our own agendas. In many ways we decide to what extent issues of justice will be explicit and/or implicit. The more influence we have the more frequently we might have to remind ourselves that we are but servants of the liturgy and of the word of God. But as we become convinced of this fact, we realize, along with Mark Searle, that "Like the word of God in history, the liturgy is the revelation of God's justice in both event and word."

Justice, Power, and Praise

THEA BOWMAN, F.S.P.A.

We're talking this morning, Church, about liturgy and social justice. And I want to remind you of what Philip Franckiewitz has said: "Liturgical worship, to be authentic, must be linked to conversion and the practice of the gospel in our personal and communal lives." When we talk about justice, that's all we're talking about—the practice of the gospel.

Some of us think that social justice is something we bring to liturgy from time to time. But Eucharist is a proclamation of the Good News. And what's good news when you're hungry? What's good news when you're homeless? What's good news when you're thirsty? What's good news when your world is torn apart by war? What's good news when your land is exploited by capitalistic corporations that claim to be helping?

And so we come together here, calling one another to faith and hope and love and conversion, and remembering the words of Jesus: "The Spirit of the Lord has been given to me for he has anointed me. He has sent me to bring Good News to the poor; to proclaim liberty to captives; and to the blind, new sight; to set the downtrodden free; and to proclaim the Lord's year of favor," here and now.

One of the reasons some of our liturgies are tired and ineffective (young folks say they're boring!) is that we begin without really gathering. The first act of liturgy is the gathering together of the people of God. How many of you have been to a liturgy where they attempted to proceed before that first act of worship, that first act of liturgy, the bonding of minds and hearts and goals and purposes and faith and love and joy, the leaning on the promise that where two or three of us are gathered in Jesus' name, he's going to be with us, the celebration of our realization that we are brothers and sisters gathered in Jesus' name, the joy of reaching out to touch somebody?

Clarence Joseph Rivers said, "The Catholic Church has good rituals and ceremonies, but they are done without style, without beauty, and without grace." So often we attempt to do liturgy without bonding. You come into a silent church—and I'm not talking about the silence of prayer—you come into this silent church: nobody looks at you, nobody acknowledges your presence, nobody welcomes you, nobody includes you, nobody smiles at you, nobody touches you. I've seen people come to church, stay in church, and leave church without any human contact. Sometimes we come together in the same church without becoming one people.

We come together in the same church: black people, red people, brown people, yellow people, white people, and all the colors and hues and tones that God so graciously created in between. We come together in the same church: rich and poor, literate, educated, urbane and illiterate, street people and folks who wear Gucci, young babies and the elders who have borne the heat of the day, new immigrants, refugees, people who are frustrated and lonely and alienated and disenfranchised and dispossessed.

We all come into our churches together. And so often

we do not see or reach out or touch one another. We surround ourselves with invisible barriers and boundaries that somehow only admit people who look like we do, walk like we do, talk like we do, think like we do, pray like we do. ("You know, I really can't pray with them; they're charismatic." And then the charismatic folks say, "Well I can't—you know, the Spirit really is not there.") Have you seen it? I know it's negative, but you've experienced it and I've experienced it.

The table of the Lord is designed to be a welcome table where we reach out and touch one another across the customary barriers and boundaries, across race and sex and class, elitism, defeatism, holier-than-thouism. You know how some folks are: They'll come in and they'll say, "Well, perhaps it was entertaining, but there wasn't much cognitive data." You know they say that?! I just want to make sure you're understanding me.

If you go to a real black church, they promise you that you will have a good time in church. One reason why some of us go to church and stay so long is that we're having a good time. Now that means that if you are in sorrow, you will find comfort and consolation. If you are in grief, you will find someone to share your burden. If you are tired, you will find rest. If you are burdened, you will find relaxation and relief. If you've got a tear, you'll find joy.

An old lady says, "I go to church, I put my burden down at the door. I ain't no fool. I know I've got to pick it up, but I've got to get me some strength. I've got to get me some relief. In the time of sorrow, he will hide me."

The Church is about justice, every liturgy about justice, every day about justice. The liturgy that is not in union with the whole Church is not authentic. Would you buy that?

The majority of the people in the Catholic Church are not middle-class white folks. The majority of people in the Catholic Church are people of color. Be sure your constituents understand this. The majority of the people in the Catholic Church, by your standards and mine, are poor. There are more Catholics in Africa right now than in North America. There are more Catholics in tiny Central America than in Eastern Europe. There are more Catholics in South America than in Western Europe. The Church is growing faster in Asia than in North America.

So the changed complexion of the College of Cardinals is merely reflective of the complexion of the Church of the Lord Jesus Christ. The liturgy that is not in union with the whole Church is not authentic. And when we consider that the majority of the people in the Church are poor, that the majority of the people in the Church are suffering, the liturgy must be for all of us: healing and comfort and bonding and joy.

The Eucharist is a celebration of a community in union with Jesus. Jesus makes the gift of himself to all the people: the ones you don't like, the ones you think aren't quite worthy, the ones you don't speak to because you don't see them when you pass them by on the street. Eucharist is Jesus offering all, all of us to the Father in complete giving.

When we come to liturgy, we're called to conversion—conversion in the Spirit of joy. We've got to get right. So we have the penitential rite as a part of every liturgy that we celebrate together. The act of penitence is a call to justice, a call to redress of grievances, a call to forgiveness as we are forgiven; a call to love the Lord with my whole heart and my whole soul and my mind and all my strength; and to love my neighbor as myself.

For the times I refused or ignored or did not see my sister's and brother's pain—Lord have mercy, Lord have mercy, Lord have mercy.

For the times I bypassed the sick and lonely, the frustrated and the poor—Lord have mercy, Lord have mercy, Lord have mercy.

For the time I condemned the addict, the derelict, the criminals, the victim of AIDS, without knowing or understanding—Lord have mercy, Lord have mercy, Lord have mercy.

For the times I contributed to the violence of the world—Lord have mercy, Lord have mercy, Lord have mercy.

For the times I failed to confront the violence in my own heart, attitudes, and behavior—Lord have mercy, Lord have mercy, Lord have mercy.

For the times I nourished or tolerated or profited from racism or sexism, militarism, materialism, consumerism, clericalism, elitism, defeatism, holier-than-thouism—Lord have mercy, Lord have mercy, Lord have mercy.

For the times I knew and understood, but failed to speak out—Lord have mercy, Lord have mercy, Lord have mercy.

For the times I did not know because I did not see my sister's or my brother's pain—Lord have mercy, Lord have mercy, Lord have mercy.

And having declared our penitence and our contrition, we wash it away in the healing and cleansing water so that we can come forth cleansed, so that we can come forth healed, so that we can come forth renewed.

When you commit yourself to justice, God's going to come to the water. Your mama, your daddy won't know you. The world will turn against you, but you will be cleansed and healed.

Having faced within our own hearts the injustice, we can

truly say, "Glory to God in the highest, and peace to all God's people." We say that prayer of peace. Sometimes we say it glibly. It's a prayer of peace. It's a proclamation of peace. It's a commitment to peace. And everybody knows that without justice, there can be no peace.

I stand for justice. I commit myself to justice. I commit my heart and my behavior. I refuse to tolerate or profit from unjust structures and institutions. I pledge myself daily to work for justice. I can't do everything, but I can do something. Day after day after day I can make my commitment.

Before you go to bed at night, examine your conscience—what have I done this day for justice? What have I done this day to help somebody who is oppressed? You know, the biggest way to help the oppressed, folks, is to get your feet off their necks. Go yourself to Pharaoh. (In my time you don't want to do that. Because if you go in there to Pharaoh, Pharaoh's going to rip your butt!)

"Glory to God in the highest and peace. . ." From the Gloria we move to the Liturgy of the Word. We're supposed to be celebrating the Word every time we have liturgy. But that's dull and tiring, too, sometimes. What's the sense of you getting up and mumbling something if your proclamation of the Word does not speak justice to my heart and my soul and my mind? You might as well give me the book and let me read it myself.

In other words, when we proclaim justice, we've got to proclaim justice so that the folks sitting in the pews hear justice; to proclaim the Word in the assembly so that the people can hear and respond to the Good News. And the Good News is love.

I think the Old Testament is written for liturgists. "I hate, I spurn your feasts, I take no pleasure in your solemnities;

your cereal offerings I will not accept; nor consider your peace offerings. Away with your noisy songs. I will not listen to the melodies of your harps. But if you would offer me holocaust, then let justice surge like water and goodness like an unfailing stream." Then we will come to church and really have a good time.

We will find shelter for the homeless. We will feed the hungry, comfort the lonely, visit the incarcerated, teach the illiterate, live our concerns for the elderly poor. We will listen to people who hurt. We will live our concern for the declining earnings of working women, for inadequate child care, for the fact that over 14 percent of all Americans live below the poverty line; that the poverty rate for children under six is 24 percent; that one out of every four children lives in poverty; and among blacks and Hispanics, the percentage is even greater.

We'll be intolerant of racism, intolerant of racism and sexism and classism and clericalism and elitism and defeatism and materialism and consumerism and all those other kinds of isms that lead us to injustice and to destruction. We will use our spiritual, moral, social, economic, political, and diplomatic power to work for justice.

We will deal seriously with the whole policy of American intervention. We're supposed to be out there helping folks, and we so often end up exploiting people. We'll really deal with the military policy. Think what would happen if every time we came to church and celebrated liturgy we would really, really take seriously our justice commitment.

Think about the Ethiopians who are starving to death; think about death squads in our Latin American nations; think about apartheid in South Africa that goes on and on and on. We ask ourselves in Jesus' name, how do we challenge the oppressive structures in this global community, this country, this world, this Church? How do we work and struggle and share leadership and decision-making in such a way that the presence of justice in our hearts, in our families, in our nations, in our world, is a felt reality?

Our world is in trouble, and in this time of trouble the proclamation of the new law is compelling. "For God so loved the world that he gave his only begotten Son so that whosoever believeth in him will not perish but have everlasting life." Those who prefer a cognitive approach can get ready for the equation. Jesus said: "As my Father has loved me, I also love you" and "As I have loved you also, so you should love one another. Greater love than this nobody has than to lay down life." Lay down life! Sometimes we think we've done enough.

Let's talk a moment about social justice and the pulpit. So often, you know, the pulpit doesn't seem to be serious about justice for everyone, life and love and responsibility for everyone. How often do you hear talk from the pulpit about violence, about international and national violence, about crime in our streets, about abuse, about child abuse and wife abuse and parent abuse, even husband abuse?

How often do you hear talk from the pulpit about physical and emotional and mental abuse, the kind that we find in some of "the best" of our Catholic families? How often do you hear talk from the pulpit about greed, about using other people as steppingstones to further your career, about materialism?

We've got Catholic Christian people—I'm talking about some "good" Catholics — who don't have time. Husband doesn't have time to talk to wife; wife doesn't have time to talk to husband; they don't have time to deal with the children. You-all weren't raised like that. How often do you hear from the pulpit about injustice in the home and family? How often do you hear that relationship without responsibility is unjust?

How often do you hear from the pulpit the serious injunctions about racism or sexism or classism? Racism is bad, but look at classism. All these folks look like one another. Some of them come from the same family, and they can't respect each other because this one's got more money or property or influence or style.

And if the sermon is not about justice, what's it about? If you don't want to talk about justice from the pulpit, then talk about love. Be positive. Talk about loving your neighbor as yourself. Talk about doing the work of Jesus. Talk about being the Church; it's the same thing. Talk about Jesus and the lame, the deaf, the blind, the lepers. All the categories are still around. Talk about the paralyzed and the dead that Jesus restored to life. We're supposed to be giving sight to the blind, healing the sick, cleansing the lepers, raising the dead. That's the work of justice.

If you don't want to talk about justice, just call it love. Love somebody. Love somebody into health. Love somebody into life. Preach justice and teach justice every Sunday. And get rid of the tired, poor, theoretical, worn-out homilies.

When we have celebrated the Word, then we say, "I believe." You know—I believe in God the Father of us all. I believe in God the Son who died for all. I believe in the Spirit who unites us all. I believe in the holy catholic Church, the holy universal Church. I believe in the forgiveness of sins and everlasting life. I believe in faith. I believe in my call to defend life and protect life and restore life.

There is a creed that I love. It's by Ka Pepe Diokno:

I believe in Jesus Christ, who came to encourage us and to heal us, to deliver us from oppressors, to proclaim the peace of God to all. He has given himself to the world; the Lord lives among all people; he is among us as the Living God.

I believe in the Church called to be a light for all nations, urged by the Spirit to serve all people.

I do not believe in the right of the strongest, nor the force of arms, nor the power of oppressors.

I want to believe in human rights, in the solidarity of all people, and the power of nonviolence.

I do not believe in racism, in wealth, privilege, or the established order. I want to believe that all women and men are equal; and that order based on violence and injustice is not order.

I do not believe we can ignore things which happen far away. I want to believe that the whole world is my home, and that the field that I plow and the harvest I reap belong to everyone.

I do not believe that I can fight oppression far away if I tolerate injustice here.

I want to believe that there is but one right everywhere; that I am not free if even one person remains enslaved. I do not believe that war and hunger are inevitable, and peace unattainable.

I want to believe in the beauty of simplicity, in love with open hands, in genuine peace on earth—in our time.

I do not believe that all suffering is in vain, nor that our dreams will remain but dreams, nor that death is the end.

But I dare to believe always and in spite of everything in a new humanity; in God's dream of a new heaven which is a new earth where genuine peace will flourish because there is justice.

Having shared our belief, we are willing and ready to make our offering: bread and wine, ourselves in union, the suffering Church with the victims of injustice, with our brothers and sisters in South Africa and Poland and Nicaragua and El Salvador and Cuba and Hungary and Russia and right here.

I offer myself just as I am. You might not think I'm much, but I'm all I've got and I'm all that I'm going to get. And your offering of me is a part of your gift to the Father. To own me, to accept me, to love me through it all, to accept one another in Jesus' name, that's justice.

I'm imperfect and incomplete; God is not through with me yet. But in union with you and in union with Jesus, I offer all that I am and all that I have. I can't do it by myself anymore. You can't do it by yourself. We offer together as Church.

Having offered ourselves with love and in love, we are ready for Eucharist, for the breaking of bread, for the consecration of bread and wine, for the consecration of all that we have and all that we are. Our communion is the communion of Jesus with the Father, the communion of the Father with Jesus, the communion of Jesus with us, the communion of us with Jesus, the communion of us with one another.

You know the Scripture. If you go to the altar and you remember you've got something against your sister or brother, you leave your gift at the altar and go make peace. That's about justice! Then we come together in Jesus' name to break bread together as a sign of our acceptance of Jesus, as a sign of our acceptance of one another, as a sign of our commitment to the work of salvation.

Children of one heavenly Father coming together from Asia and Africa and North America and South America and

Europe and Australia; coming together rich and poor; educated and illiterate; urbane and sophisticated; frustrated, lonely, homeless, alienated, tired and destitute, to break together the bread of life, to praise the Lord together.

The quest for justice demands that I walk in ways that I never walked before, that I talk and think and pray and learn and grow in ways that are new to me. If I'm going to share faith with my brothers and sisters who are Chinese or Jamaican or South African or Winnebago Indian, I've got to learn new ways and new means, new languages, new rituals, new procedures, new understandings, so I can read my brother's heart, so I can hear my sister's call, and I can live justly.

I don't like to talk about liturgy and social justice. I don't like to talk about liturgy. I think too many folks spend too much time talking about liturgy and too little time really celebrating liturgy. I mean some real stomp-down celebration that leaves you spent and tired because you have given every ounce of energy from your whole being, because you have shared so much of faith, hope, love, and joy.

I don't like to talk about social justice either. There's too much talk about social justice. We get in special trouble when we talk about social justice to people who are poor, to people who are oppressed, to people who are hungry. They hear us talking and they think that our conversation means commitment and conviction.

A lot of our churches do not, on a regular daily basis, work for justice. If we're serious about social justice, it means that every night before sleep I raise the question "What have I done this day to make my world more just?"

Whether my justice benefits the child or the elder, my sister in South Africa, or my mother in El Salvador is immaterial. The question is "What have I done this day that has changed things?"

Love is difficult. Love is demanding. Some folks think that Jesus did a great thing for us when he hung three hours on the cross and died for us. I think that was the easy part. I think the hard part was when the almighty Word leapt down, when God became human, became baby, became child, became man, and walked this earth with us for thirty-three years giving and loving and doing justice every day. After all that, three hours on the cross was little or nothing!

If we are to be serious about the work of justice, it means we have to put on the Lord Jesus Christ. You can't do it by yourself. You get so tired; you get so discouraged; you give out and you give up; you burn out. Liturgy is the act of the people of God. And so in liturgy, in the public hearing, we make a public commitment to God.

If we're serious about social justice, and if we love one another in Jesus' name, when we see each other neglect that commitment—lag, stumble, or fall—we have to call and challenge one another to justice. ("I heard that you only paid your secretary $3.35 an hour. How long has she been working for you?" Look how Church folks sometimes pay the cooks and even some of the religious educators and musicians!)

If we challenge one another as brothers and sisters in Jesus, if the little children learn they have to challenge us when they see us engaged in attitudes and behaviors that seem to be oppressive and unjust, we'll grow in awareness; we'll live each day more justly.

Sometimes we do the damage inadvertently. Sometimes we're just afraid to speak out. That's one reason why in our liturgy we exchange the sign of peace. It's supposed to be real, intentional. We give peace. We become peacemakers. We accept one another with open eyes and open arms and open hearts. We accept one another with all our weaknesses, failures, and inconsistencies. We help one another to love freely, to live justly, to walk holily before the Lord.

Sometimes we fall into blaming: blame the priest, blame the bishop, blame the pope, blame the DRE, blame the musicians, blame the liturgy director, even blame the little children, blame your mama. We are the Church! If we assume our real responsibilities as Christians, if we assume our real responsibilities to work for justice, we shall overcome: overcome poverty, overcome hunger, overcome homelessness, overcome the frustrations that lead to crime, overcome drug problems, overcome the violence in our homes and streets, in our nation and world.

But every time we come to liturgy, we've got to be serious about our commitment to justice. We have come together in Jesus' name to celebrate our call to justice, our call to peace. And as in every liturgy, let us bless one another and go in Jesus' name.

Let us go, revived and renewed!

Let us go to do justice!

Liturgy and Social Justice: Past Relationships and Future Possibilities

J. BRYAN HEHIR

My task here is to examine the past and future relationship of the liturgical life of the Church—the liturgy of the Church—and social ministry and social justice in the Church. And so I will proceed to that task in three steps. I want to look at what I'll call the *road* to Vatican II, the relationship of liturgy and social justice. Secondly, I'll look at the *event* of Vatican II, liturgy and social justice. And then I want to look at the postconciliar period, both as history and as future challenge on liturgy and social justice.

First, the road to Vatican II—liturgy and social justice. The Second Vatican Council was a central event for liturgists and for those in the social ministry of the Church. My proposition is that there are lessons for both those who have the responsibility for the life of the liturgy in the Church and for those who have social ministry responsibilities. There are lessons for both of us, not only in what the Council said, but in how we got to the Council—how the Council came to be.

So let me offer an interpretation of how the Council came to be and, within that interpretation, look at the relationship of liturgy and social justice leading to Vatican II.

My proposition begins with the assertion that the Council neither dropped from Heaven nor emerged from Hell. There are interpretations that both of those happened, but I want to reject them both at the outset. The Council was indeed part of a process; but although it was part of a process, the Council was not inevitable. At the core of the Council was an act of leadership. Leadership by definition is the capacity to see a future that is not predetermined and to give that future a direction by a decision that shapes the future.

John XXIII took the Church as it was, with a historical process developing that could create a council, but John XXIII catalyzed the Council. So the Council was not inevitable, but the Council was not totally new. A catalytic act of leadership stands at the origin of the Council. That catalytic act of leadership, of calling the Council, however, was able to build upon a process, a historical process that was at work in Catholicism. Essentially, my argument is that the raw material for the Council had been in progress for fifty to one hundred years. Without the catalytic act of leadership, that whole process might not have been brought to fruition the way it has.

But on the other hand, while one wants to compliment John XXIII as highly as one can, it is the case that he has catalyzed something that was already there to be catalyzed. The raw material existed.

Let me argue the proposition this way: Take six of the major documents of the Council—the document on the Church *(Lumen Gentium)*, the document on the Church in the world, the document on ecumenism, the document on the liturgy, the document on revelation, and the document on religious freedom—six of the sixteen documents of Vatican II. I would argue that it is possible to document a fifty to one hundred-year history for each one of them. Take each text in isolation and you move back through fifty to a hundred years of preparation.

Involved in the history of each of those texts are two things: There are individuals that are absolutely crucial, and there are movements made up of individuals who are crucial and other individuals who are essential but not crucial in the same way.

The individuals particularly to be highlighted are theologians whose work prepared directly for the Council. In all honesty, at a time in the Church when theologians have not the most simple life in the world today, it is important to look at this period before the Council. For the litany of names that leads to the Council goes beyond John XXIII. It goes to Congar, De Lubac, Murray, Danielou—every single one of them in trouble. Every single one of them lived at the edge of the life of the Church for twenty and thirty years before the Council. But it really is impossible to think about the Council in the shape we know it without those individuals.

Secondly, individuals by themselves did not create the raw material for the Council. There were movements. Individuals were part of a process. One thinks of Congar in the ecumenical movement in Paris. One thinks of the liturgical movement in the United States, in Collegeville or in other places. One thinks about the social action movement in Chicago, John A. Ryan, George Higgins. One can highlight the work of movements around each of the major texts of the Council.

Now the character of those movements leading up to Vatican II had certain specific dimensions. The movements generally were small. They did not involve large numbers of people. Individuals in those movements lived at the edge of the life of the Church as theologians. They lived within the Church, but at the edge. Being at the edge meant they were often in trouble. They also lived at the edge with a vision. What kept them alive in the midst of the trouble was a vision of what the Church might be. And that vision meant that they always saw themselves as part of a movement whose task was to penetrate the life of a whole Church. Within these movements they lived not in a sectarian way, but they moved and lived with the sense of being a leaven, and they sought to penetrate the whole.

For the people in those movements, the movements themselves provided certain things. They provided a sense of community that your vision was not an aberration—that others shared it. They provided a sense of reinforcement—you came together to cultivate the vision and to test it. And they provided a common task—a sense that you were in this movement because the life of the whole Church needed the piece of the truth that you thought you had in your vision. Now for each of these areas—ecclesiology, ecumenism, liturgy, social justice—I submit that if you have the time, you can trace the movement and you can trace the individuals who were central to the movement.

Let me examine specifically the relationship between liturgy and social justice on the road to Vatican II. Just a personal note: I came to the social ministry of the Church through reading the proceedings of the Liturgical Conference. I had always had a political interest before I entered the seminary. But my seminary experience drove me to the liturgy under the guidance of Shawn Sheehan, who taught me that in the midst of the liturgical movement there developed the social vision of the Church.

I remember my first year in the seminary. Bill Leonard came from Boston College and gave a talk in which he said there were three pieces of the life of the Church that needed to be woven together by anyone studying for the priesthood: *Mystici Corporis, Mediator Dei,* and the social encyclicals. Leonard said that *Mystici Corporis* was the Church in itself, that *Mediator Dei* was the Church at prayer, and the social encyclicals were the Church at work. Not a bad vision to live with.

What surrounded this vision was the sense of the Church. It was an ecclesial vision. And so it was that the Council was an ecclesial Council. Vatican II was not a Christological council, not a Trinitarian council. Vatican II fulfilled the prediction of one of those theologians, Henri De Lubac, who said that this was the century of the Church, and indeed, in the midst of the century of the Church there emerged the event of the Council.

Specifically in this ecclesial vision, there was the linkage of liturgy and social ministry, or what we called at that time—social action. The linkage was clear in the people who were part of the movement. The liturgists lived with a sense that you could not be the Church if you weren't social; and the people in the social ministry lived with the sense that the source of what you did in terms of social justice rested in what you were as the Church, and that was specified when the Church came together during prayer.

And that theoretical linkage took shape in practice. The Church's social ministry of the 1930s and 1940s was in the labor movement, and the labor priests and the liturgy were closely connected. I remember when the call went out from Selma, when I was still in seminary. The priests who went to Selma from my diocese were the people who were involved in the liturgical movement—Sheehan, Tom Carroll, and others.

So, you had a linkage in both theory and practice that led to the Council. Let me then turn to the Council and what happened there.

I've so far argued that you couldn't have the Council unless you had this preceding history, that the preceding history is a documented relationship between the Church at prayer and the Church in social witness, and that that relationship prepared the way for a coming together of themes at the Council that really shaped the Catholic vision in a particular way.

So let me look at the Council. My view of the Council in this lecture is the same view that Rahner offers, that is, to see the Council as both the culmination of a process and the beginning of a new process, that the Council is neither an end in itself nor a beginning in itself. But the Council came from somewhere, crystallized the vision, and then set you out on a new vision. But one has to understand what came together at the Council, before we get direction of where we proceed from there.

If you look at the Council from the perspective of the liturgy and social ministry, the Council meant different things for each side of that equation. What I will do is to comment on what it meant for each side of the liturgy/social ministry equation, and then later on I discuss the consequences of the Council for both liturgy and social ministry.

In discussing the Council and its document on the liturgy (I'm too experienced a speaker to come before a group of liturgists and exegete the document on the liturgy), I will confine myself to general comments that by definition will be safe.

In a sense, if you look at the document on the liturgy of Vatican II, one way to describe it is to say that the history I've described has produced its product; that in a sense the liturgical movement and all that went before it had prepared the way so well for Vatican II that the document of the Council was an event waiting to happen.

Another way to describe it is to say that when you know the history of the liturgical movement, and then you read the document of the Council, there are no surprises. That happened with other documents of the Council: anyone who had read Congar carefully is not surprised by *Lumen Gentium;* it's almost embarrassing, it's so clear; anyone who had read John Courtney Murray carefully is even more embarrassed when reading the document on religious liberty—embarrassed in the sense that Council documents are supposed to be the product of everybody. But this one person's ideas are so clear in the document that it becomes clear how things led to the Council.

But the document on the liturgy was a victory, if you will, for the themes that had been pressed for so many years: that the liturgical event is an event of all the baptized; that participation is the key; how, both in style and substance, the liturgy would be celebrated and how we understand or how we should understand it. In a sense, it seems to me the conciliar document is a clear-cut product of the previous forty to fifty years, maybe even longer. And a clear-cut victory for those who had lived at the edge of the Church with a vision and sought to penetrate the whole Church with that vision.

Moreover, the style of the document and its implementation opened a process that, in the sense that the Council is a beginning of a process to be implemented, was also there.

Indeed for most Catholics the implementation of the conciliar vision of the liturgy is their primary experience of Vatican II. Their primary experience of Vatican II was the day they walked into church and the priest was looking at them, and maybe nobody told them the previous Sunday that he was going to be. But then the whole question about how that could happen becomes the primary experience—not the only one—but the primary way in which people sense the Council entering their life.

So in one sense the document on the liturgy stresses continuity with what prepared for it. No surprises. The document is both a reaching back into the life of the Church, a restoration of the liturgical life of the Church, and an act of creative renewal that opens new possibilities for the future.

If one looks at the Council document that is the social ministry document, the social justice document—*Gaudium et Spes*—there is some similarity, but there are also some differences. There was continuity between what *Gaudium et Spes* said and the movement prior to it, the social action movement of the social encyclicals. But unlike the document on the liturgy, I would argue that *Gaudium et Spes* contains some surprises, that even if you had known the history leading up to Vatican II, you would not have predicted *Gaudium et Spes*.

First, there is the surprise of the text itself. In the planning for Vatican II there was no doubt that there would be a document on the liturgy, no doubt that there would be a document on the Church, and no doubt, even, that there would be a document on ecumenism. But the fact of the matter is, there was no plan for the document *Gaudium et Spes*. The original drafts of the Council had as their only explicitly ecclesial document *Lumen Gentium*.

What happens, first of all, in the Council, is what is supposed to happen in councils. That is to say, that the event is larger than what people plan for, that there's a dynamic to the conciliar experience itself that carries a council beyond what was planned. And so if one looks at the dynamic of Vatican II, one of the experiences of the Council is that the bishops come to an insight that they never plan for. They come to the insight that you can't describe the life of the Church only within the context of the subject matter of *Lumen Gentium,* that that internal reflection on the life of the Church is both essential to Catholicism and inadequate for a definition of what the Church is. It's interesting to watch the dynamic of the Council. In *Lumen Gentium* and in the document on the liturgy you get hints that you must drive outside the Church or beyond the Church in order to encompass the full definition of the Church. The text on the liturgy opens with what could easily be called a sense of the signs of the times as they would be described in *Gaudium et Spes.* But the reference is passing. The reference is understandably brief, but you get a sense that one tries to situate the celebration of the prayer of the Church within an awareness of what the world is like; but it's passing. Then you take *Lumen Gentium,* and it talks about the Church as the sacrament of unity in the world. But then so is the subject matter of *Lumen Gentium* the internal life of the Church.

You get a hint in both the document on the liturgy and the document on the Church that to some degree the subject matter of the texts is more contained than the vision that moves them. But what was the Council to do? For there was no plan to move beyond the vision, good as it was, of the internal life of the Church.

And so one sensed the dynamic of the Council when at

the end of the first session, after having discussed, debated, and shaped both *Lumen Gentium* and the document on the liturgy, three bishops stood up—and Montini was one of them—and said that everything they had done was necessary and good, and yet it was inadequate. For the world wants to know what the Church of Christ *is* for it. The world wants to know what the Church of Christ *is* in shaping the history of which we are a part.

And out of those interventions came a decision of the Council to create a document they had never planned for, to create a document on the Church in the world. That decision, at one and the same time, declared *Lumen Gentium* to be only a partial ecclesiology, and it declared the complementary nature of *Lumen Gentium* and what would become *Gaudium et Spes*.

So the first surprise is that the text itself emerged from the Council. The second surprise is the substance of the text itself. It is not really simply a straight line drawn out of the social encyclicals. *Gaudium et Spes* moves beyond the encyclicals—the social encyclicals—in both substance and style. In substance it moves beyond them, because the encyclicals tended to be primarily moral analyses of social issues—understandably.

But *Gaudium et Spes* is more than that. The lasting part of *Gaudium et Spes* is not part two, its analysis of the issues. The lasting part of *Gaudium et Spes* is part one—its ecclesiological reflection. This is primarily an ecclesial document. And what it does is to take the social ministry and put it at the center of the Church's life, where the liturgy already lived, but where the social ministry did not live.

Those in the social ministry had lived on the edge in a particular way: they had always spent half their lives justifying their existence in the life of the Church. And now, after *Gaudium et Spes,* that task is no longer necessary.

And so the fundamental move is not a moral analysis, it's not an issue; it's an ecclesiological move of centering the social ministry at the heart of the life of the Church. And you can trace this move in its consequences in the life of the Church since the Council, for you can go from *Gaudium et Spes* to *Justice in the World* five years later, and then to Paul VI's *Evangelii Nunitandi* of 1975, and then to *Redemptor Hominis* of John Paul II—a move that deepens the sense that the Church must be social if it is to be a Church; that the social is not optional, is not marginal, is not the choice of a few; that it grows essentially out of the nature and ministry of the Church as the Church's prayer does.

The substance of the document is complemented by the surprise of style. The social encyclicals tended to use a classical, natural-law analysis of issues. That style is insightful. It continues to be necessary, but *Gaudium et Spes* takes all of that and situates it in a biblical, ecclesiological, Christological context. So once again the social ministry of the Church is not looked upon as a kind of conclusion one draws from Christian faith. It is situated right at the center of where we shape our vision of the faith: Christologically, ecclesiologically, and biblically.

Once you come away from Vatican II with the end product of these histories of movements that led to the Council, and then the creative act of the Council itself, you come away with again, I submit, an ecclesial vision that says the Catholic Church is scriptural, sacramental, and social; that you must hold the three together to be the Church.

So the movements that preceded the Council, the individuals that gave insight to the movements, and the event of the Council itself produced both a synthesis of what had gone before and a breakthrough that was unexpected, as you bring together this vision of the Church as scriptural, sacramental, and social.

Now one comes to the postconciliar period. My purpose here is to do two things: to comment on the postconciliar process of the linkage of liturgy and social ministry, and to pose a postconciliar challenge to look at what potential there is, and what problems there are, for those who are faithful to a vision that says the Church is sacramental, social, and scriptural.

First, the process since the Council. Here again I have to go back and speak in broad terms that are open to criticism, but I think the general direction is adequate. The general direction can be sustained, although the critique would have to be handled point by point. Essentially, what I've argued is that the Council is a major achievement of both synthesis and insight; that the raw material of the ecclesial vision—scriptural, sacramental, and social—was there, but it had to be crystallized. It had to be put together, and it had to be centered in the life of the Church. And that was an act of both intelligence and authoritative declaration. In our polity you need both. If you have only insight but don't receive legitimation, then the question is: Are the insights for everyone or just for a few? If you have authoritative legitimation without insight, then you're in even more trouble. So the Council was a happy combination of what you need in Catholicism to give direction to the life of the Church: insight and legitimation.

One then moves from that substantive judgment to the process of the postconciliar period. And here it gets complicated because, in a sense, the victory for the movements resulted in a disbursal of the movements. It is not an un-known phenomenon. You capture city hall, and there is the sense that the task is complete; that the vision you had at the edge now belongs to everyone; therefore, explicit culti-vation of the vision, the kind of daily work that preceded the Council, is presumed not to be necessary because now everybody owns the vision. It's been legitimated.

My point here is not an argument that says that the post-conciliar period ought to look like the preconciliar period. The task is different, but the explicit cultivation of differ-ent dimensions of the total vision and the explicit cultiva-tion of the linkage, in our case of liturgy and social ministry, did not happen as it needed to happen. There are all kinds of reasons for that. To some degree, the implementation of each piece of the vision exhausted available energy.

Secondly, one must situate this historically. The social agenda exploded on Catholicism right as the Council con-vened. So Catholicism of the 1960s and 70s was a Catholi-cism dealing with a dual explosion in the society itself and in the life of the Church.

My point is to look at this postconciliar process in order to look at the future, because we are coming up on the twenty-fifth anniversary of Vatican II in 1990, and by that time we ought to look at where we are: that we will have in our memory the preconciliar period; that we will have lived through the event of the Council and the postconciliar experience; and that we are sufficiently far enough away from the Council to really recognize the postconciliar experience as a time in itself with its own tasks—and now there's an-other time.

How these areas of linkage that preceded the Council were crystallized in the Council and are still in need of cultivation, how that ought to be carried forward in this post-conciliar period is precisely a task that again needs intelligence, intuition, learning, dedicated movements, and new legitimation. That means one needs to at least sketch out this challenge. So let me talk less about what happened in the postconciliar period and talk about how I define the challenge that needs to be thought about as we approach the twenty-fifth anniversary of Vatican II.

I think the way to do this is to learn from *Gaudium et Spes* and to start with the signs of the times and then reflect upon the ecclesial vision in light of those signs. So as one experiment with the signs of the times, let me say a word about situating the Church in American society.

The Council teaches us that to define the Church is to define us as a community and an institution. We are both. We ought to claim both. We ought to see both as a potential. It doesn't always work that way. Sometimes the community is a burden and sometimes the institution is a burden.

But the potential of Catholicism rests with the capability of combining community and institution. Outside observers tell us that. Robert Bellah, from Berkeley, reflecting upon the experience of the pastoral letters of the Council and reflecting upon the state of American society and habits of the heart, says to Catholics, "Don't forget what you have." In a society as large as this, it takes a large community and institution to move it. And there are very few societies that combine both vision and institutional structure. While we might not always live out both of them well, both of them are there to be used.

As a community, we're the largest single religious community in the country—55 million people. As an institution, we are present in every significant place where a society gets touched and moved: where people are educated; where people are healed and health care is given; where social service is provided; where immigrants are brought into a society; and most of all, present in that creation that we take for granted—the parish. We have more parishes than the Postal Service has post offices. We are present every place where the society comes together. Any social scientist will tell you that is valuable. If you can open up a local chapter on every square inch of turf in the society you want to touch, that's not a bad start.

But it's more complicated than that. We are not only a large community with a substantial social structure. We are a large and complicated community. The classical description of Catholicism since the Council is that we are now a post-immigrant community. The argument is that the election of John Kennedy and the event of the Council itself have taken what had been an immigrant Church since the middle of the nineteenth century and brought it to the center of American society. I think that's true, but it's only half the story.

The interesting thing about us today is that we are both a post-immigrant Church and a newly immigrant Church. The immigrants today don't come from Eastern Europe and Northern Europe and the British Isles; they come from Central America and Latin America and East Asia. But the post-immigrant part is true. For good or ill, we are at the very center of American society. Not just in our institutions but in our community. Every major place that you think of where this society makes decisions about where it's going to go, we are there for good or ill. In the United States Congress Catholics outnumber any other religious community three to one. *Fortune* magazine tells us there are more Catholic chief executive officers than any other religious group in the country. The labor movement has always been filled with Catholics. The university world still has a way to go, but we are in a very different place than when John Ellis talked about it in his famous address in the middle 1950s. There is no major place in American society where Catholics are not present.

So the post-immigrant part is true. But the newly immigrant part is also true. There is almost no other institution in American society that is both at the center and at the edge again. And that's an interesting place to be if you can put it together as one community.

So in a society faced with creating a common vision out of many voices, faces, races, and cultures, the Church is a microcosm of that. We don't even have to work at it; it's just there. What we do with it is part of the challenge. And how we bring that community together to pray is always a critical test moment. How much our prayer reflects the complexity of the community and the possibility of the community and what we do with it is crucial. Because obviously the way we pray is preceded by the way we live as a parish and as a Church. The way we pray should shape the way we live as this diverse, unique community.

The social challenge facing that community is also interesting to sketch because it will take us from *Gaudium et Spes* to the pastorals of the American bishops. There would be no pastorals without *Gaudium et Spes*; that is where you see the ecclesial shift. The bishops argued about the specifics of the pastorals, but no bishop stood up on the floor and said that this was not the business of the Church. I submit that that would have happened in a Church without the Council. The argument would not have been about the tactics, the details, or the policies, but about why this document was on the agenda. And the ecclesial consensus of *Gaudium et Spes* is manifested in the fact that not one single person stood up and asked that.

But the road from *Gaudium et Spes* to the pastorals highlights the social challenge facing us. I submit that the social challenge is both our challenge of the Church within the U.S. and the challenge of how the U.S. stands in the world. What the liturgy will help us to remember is the voice of the prophets. The prophets, different though they are as individuals, always had a common sentence to speak to the community. The prophets always said that the quality of faith will be tested by the character of justice in the land. And then they pressed that sentence further and said that the character of justice in the land will be tested by the way the women, the orphans, and the aliens are treated. And it's remarkable to go from society in the eighth century B.C. to U.S. society in the late 1980s. It's remarkable to read the presence of the prophets. For the pastoral on the economy tells us that the most vulnerable people in American society are women and children. And our ministry with undocumented persons in the United States says that what the prophets called the aliens are still one of our toughest political challenges.

It's remarkable to listen to the prophets about the children. For they are even more vulnerable than the women. One out of four children is poor in the United States today. Two out of five black children are poor. Our infant mortality rate in some cities is below that of developing countries. The National Academy of Sciences tells us that on any given night in the United States 100,000 children are without shelter. Those are not runaways. Those are 100,000 children in families without shelter. The housing problem in our major urban areas makes the sheltering of the homeless such an imperative that we dare not celebrate the liturgy without saying something about it.

Thirty-seven million people in the United States live without health insurance in a society where, even when you have health insurance, it's an enormous challenge to know how you're going to care for your mother and your father or your child who gets ill.

And the difficulty is that in many ways so many other things are so good in the society. When you lived in the Depression, it was easier to keep your eye on the edge of the society because you felt that you might be close to it yourself. But when the unemployment rate is five to six percent, and when you've gone through three years of sustained economic growth, it is harder to believe that one out of four children is in poverty. It is harder to believe that 100,000 children go without shelter every night of the week. You have to work at it to keep that thought alive.

And so the voice of the prophets is precisely central to a Church that lives at the *center* of American society, where it's hard to believe that one out of four is in poverty, and it is also central to the Church that lives at the edge of American society where we know it's true.

The question becomes not only the task of the life of the internal life of the country; we also have this added other dimension, embodied in the nuclear pastoral, that states that this Church cannot confine its social ministry only to what happens within our borders. We also are a Church of one of the two superpowers of the world, so the social vision of the Church here has to also be about how we affect the rest of the world, a world whose two major characteristics are that it is nuclear in its context and increasingly inter-dependent in its content. Nuclear in its context, the abiding shadow of nuclear weapons is what lies behind the pastoral on war and peace.

What do you do? How do you think? How do you act? How do you not get petrified but act responsibly when you live in one of the two societies in the world that can call the moment of truth? The nuclear pastoral said we are the first generation since Genesis to have within our hands the capacity to threaten the creative order. The idea is not to frighten people into paralysis but simply to say that you can't live as the Church in this country and make believe that that issue is not before us. It is harder to know what to do about it, but at least we ought to not *not* say it. And the increasing interdependence of the world simply means that we live locked together in a limited world.

The whole debate in the Catholic Church of the 1980s about Central America, for example, is the case study of what we ought to be. No more conflicted issue has engaged the bishops than that of Central America, than opposing aid to the Contras, than of standing quite precisely against the general direction of U.S. policy. It is important to know that *that* community and the institution that *we* are fits us for this role.

I'll never forget, at the beginning of the decade, when Central America was just heating up. Dick Olman, professor of political science at Princeton, wrote an article in *The New York Times,* in which he said that the crucial direction of the way U.S. policy will go in Central America will depend on the Catholic Church, because it has a linkage to that area that almost no one else has. That kind of question— how the Church in the U.S. thinks about and relates to the direction of our society and the way it touches the rest of the world—is also part the social challenge for the Church.

We come back, then, to the social and liturgical challenge together. The liturgy is, theologically, obviously the center of our life in the Church. What is important to see is that the liturgy is also *socially* the center of our life. If you're going to speak to the community about housing and health care or Central America and nuclear war, the only time the community gathers in all its diversity is at the liturgy. We need specialized movements. We need specialized meetings. But at none of those will you get the whole community.

So it is socially a point of gathering. What we do there is absolutely crucial. Whether the vision is only scriptural and sacramental, or whether the vision is scriptural, sacramental, *and social,* is absolutely crucial. For people, understandably, will take their definition of what it means to be Catholic from the event that is theologically central to what we are as a Church.

I submit that when we come together the challenge is threefold. People understandably seek, I think, intelligibility, mystery, and community when they come together for the liturgy. They seek intelligibility. We are a highly secular society. We're the meaning of religion in people's lives. It's a task that consciously must be cultivated. The sense of why a person ought to believe and what difference it makes if one believes is not something we can presuppose is understood in the community. So intelligibility—how religious meaning affects life, how we should interpret life because we are believers, and what kind of direction we should give our lives is a first challenge of liturgy. Remember what Rahner said: in another age a convert could be the result of external social pressure, but in our age, every true conversion is a work of art. Every true conversion of a person to a deeper life of faith is a work of art that must be consciously chipped out of the granite of each person's life.

Intelligibility must be matched by mystery. People come not only to be informed but to experience the holy; to be touched by power. That is part of what our prayer-life does. It relativizes all of the historical forces that seem overwhelming, for one can come and be touched by a power that is transcendent and yet close to us. Intelligibility must be matched with an experience of mystery.

And both intelligibility and mystery must be communicated within a sense of community. I think one ought to not be romantic about this. I live in a parish of 10,000 people. We are not going to have an I-Thou session on Sunday morning. So I'm-okay-you're-okay is not the model here.

What a sense of community means is a sense of identity for one's personal life within a wider circle of conviction that reinforces my own sense of identity. It is a coming together that people go away from with some sense of a common task. Not that I necessarily will do it with the person who stands next to me on Sunday, whom I probably don't know, but a sense that he and I or she and I leave this place with something that holds us together. That what I believe is not some aberration but is commonly held, cultivated through the centuries, has truth, and is touched by power. No other place in the life of the Church has the possibility to combine intelligibility, mystery, and community than our celebration of the liturgy.

And so when we come together in this place, the test of the conciliar vision is at stake. A Church that is sacramental, scriptural, and social can be created at this place. The

Church at this place can be a voice; it can talk about what needs doing: sheltering the homeless, feeding the hungry, respecting the human rights of others. The Church at this place can also talk about what it ought to do, not just what others ought to do. Sheltering the homeless is a task that no diocese in this country today, in an urban area, should be without—an explicit commitment to the housing program. No Catholic health-care institution should be alive that is not consciously defining its task in terms of those who don't have health care. And thirdly, the Church can be, finally, a catalyst, because everything doesn't get done through the Church. Those people who gather on a Sunday morning must seek some sense of how they should be the Church in a thousand places this coming week, with enormously conflicted decisions to make about the way they raise their kids, do their job, vote, and act as citizens. In no other place can we be a voice, an actor, and a catalyst.

To meet this challenge as we approach the twenty-fifth anniversary of the Council, I submit we ought to think about how those two streams that together led to help create the Council—the Church at prayer and the Church in witness— ought to come together again for the post-postconciliar task.

Homily for the Closing Session

JAMES LOPRESTI, S.J.

Paris is a wonderful city! It is full of splendid monuments, rich in history, a bustling center for the arts, a feast of fine sights, enticing aromas, and exotic tastes, a celebration of human excess of just about every kind. I visited Paris for the first time last month (probably the last American Jesuit to get there!). And on one Sunday while I was there, I gathered with hundreds of other tourists from around the globe for the solemn celebration of Sunday Eucharist at the cathedral of Notre Dame. The liturgy, although perhaps a little cool, was careful, correct, dignified but not pretentious, partly in French, partly in Latin. The homily was scriptural, also careful and correct, at least insofar as I could judge, given my limited capacity to understand spoken French. My mind drifted on occasion, a sure and welcome sign that I was at Sunday Mass, a feature still as universal as Latin used to be. In fact it drifted quite a bit, and I found two particular "distractions" affecting the quality of my prayer and of my presence to that assembly of worshipers. One was the constant stream of visitors shuffling around the edge of the community, cameras in hand, heads turning left and right and craning up and down to absorb all the detail of this ancient architectural marvel. I could almost hear the Americans wondering how the medieval engineers ever figured out how to build "this thing" which is obviously bigger than "our cathedral back home." I felt a little sad as I contemplated their distance from what this assembly was about, as if in my distracted state I was any more attentive.

I also found myself focusing on the stones, those worn, dirty survivors of centuries of human inhabitation. In a mysterious way they archived a people's history. They were blackened by the smoke of millions of candles lit with an Ave and centuries of lighted coals sending up billowing incense. But all that only hinted at the deeper truth, namely, that these stones have absorbed the prayers and petitions of countless generations of worshipers. Imagine the pleas, the pain, the cries for protection from the assaults of quickly advancing armies, the horror of the Black Plague, the *Te Deums* for peace and victory, the festive coronations and royal weddings, the rampage of the Revolution, let alone the millions of littler, common folk stories of daily life struggles, such as deaths, betrayals, new hopes, blissful reveries, mystical surgings, the abuses, the delight, the awe, the reverence, all the stuff of human life—sometimes rich and full, often broken and aching, and always dreaming of what can be. Here in this high-vaulted house of worship filled with lament and petition for centuries untold, the human spirit has had the chance to soar with the surging walls and glimpse a splendidly colored vision of the possible pouring in through the noonday stained glass. Here, at least, was the chance to find communion with God and the company of saints who promised rescue and healing to a simple people, barely awakened to the power of their God-touched human spirit. The stones oozed the quietly whispered anointings of pain and anguish, of hope and yearning, rubbed into them by the scores of parishioners and pilgrims who have gathered here generation after generation.

Among other things, the stones reminded me that the cathedral of Notre Dame de Paris is a witness to human survival. War, plague, revolution, occupation have all tried their best to conquer these walls. None has finally succeeded. In fact each trauma has been the chance for the people's transformation. Each trauma has given a new reason for the people to return and pour out their hearts. Each trauma paradoxically made the stones even more holy. The vision of John on Patmos shines through: "See I make all things new," again, and again, and again—"I make all things new."

But something else is happening. Admirers now flock to the cathedral—not pilgrims any longer, but tourists. And a troubling question emerges: "Will this soul of Paris survive such aesthetic distancing?" If violence of all kind has not snuffed out the votive candles and emptied the chairs on Sunday morning, will the presentation of the building as a museum now succeed? Can "appreciation" of the awesome beauty of the place ironically signal an end to its power to gather a people and not merely harbor a collective of the curious? The tourists may prove irksome, but they are not enough of a threat to send the Parisians to the cathedral to plead in anguish for rescue from them. In fact many of the Parisians revel, if not in the presence of the tourists, at least in their adulation of anything Parisian. Was I part of the problem?

These two distractions at prayer, the stones and the tourists, have occasioned some reflections I want to share with you about liturgy and justice.

There is much concern in this assembly that our worship move our communities to work for a just social order. True worship unleashes in the community a powerful spirit which captures and convinces the heart in loving embrace of powerful stories and rich symbolic fare. Hearts surrendered in love again and again become shaped by compassion and are made vulnerable to a spirit of freedom. Such a schooling in freedom gently dissipates the energy to enslave others. This is how the liturgy is expected to form us gradually to become ambassadors of peace, workers for social reform wherever there is injustice in our world. It is subtle, powerful, and full of mystery. We know all that.

But a special caution is in order. Ours is not the only liturgy in town. The assembly of believers is not the only gathering which shapes the heart of humankind. Those tourists popping flashcubes all around the house of the Church in Paris must have another cathedral in which they surrender themselves in worship. Their presence raises some questions which we all need to face. Where else do the people of our world take their pain? Where else do the people make their pleas heard? What other walls receive their petitions? Where else do they burn their incense and light their candles? Where else do they gather with their fellows to make sense of the pain and anguish, to celebrate the victories and share the dreams? In a nutshell, where, besides at the Table of the Lord, do our people worship?

I ask all this because I think justice questions are, at root, liturgical ones, just as much as liturgical questions are justice ones. The liturgies of Lord and Taylor, Holiday Spa, and Clancy's Bar make promises to the human heart which subtly sway one into a specific way to make decisions about how life should be lived, including how others should be treated. It would be quite foolish if we who have responsibility for shaping worship in Sunday assemblies were to remain unaware of the spirit which animates the other places where people worship, and inattentive to the powerful, silent promise generated there.

The shopping mall surely is a rather banal substitute for the cathedrals of Milan, York, or Chartres. But the Saturday jaunt to Potomac Mills in suburban Washington is as close as some get to going on pilgrimage. I know; I've done it often. Unlike the tourists at Notre Dame, the shoppers at the mall are full participants at the Saturday rites. There are no back pews! The promise of prosperity is scripted into every advertisement augmented by indulgences like the Columbus Day Sale and protected by the canons of credit approval. And it all follows the liturgical calendar called the billing cycle.

Membership at the Holiday Spa elicits the promise of the delay of advancing age and forges the illusion of eternal youthfulness. The desire to look good to sexually alert others fills the humid air with each straining "exhale." No pain, no gain!

At Clancy's Bar the promise that I might not have to face aloneness, at least for tonight, and that someone really can choose me is swallowed with each sip of Campari and soda, and adds exciting flavors to the sushi.

These liturgies are elaborate, well orchestrated, and very carefully regulated. On one level they appear amusingly harmless; they are, after all, the particular foibles of our modern American sensibility. But there are subtle demons at work here. We know these promises are all rather shallow; still they have a remarkable power to influence the decisions of people about what is valuable and to be protected or sought after. They affect the daily life and well-being of ever expanding circles of people. Something powerful energized them.

The fact of the matter is that they are all liturgies of *having:* having wealth, having an attractive figure, having a partner for the night. And the liturgies of having are deeply threatened by anything that forebodes NOT having, or the possibility of losing. They are the liturgies of competition, of winners and losers, of defending our vital interests around the globe, of building stockpiles of emotional, or nuclear, weapons, of economically maneuvering all comers away from positions of threat to what we have. They come from dangerous stock, these apparently harmless rites. The world they mirror and shape is a violent and fearful one, inviting oppression and addictive behaviors.

The liturgy of the assembly of believers, by stark contrast, is meant to be a liturgy of *being:* being receivers, being chosen, being embraced in truth. They arise from an ethos so different from the liturgies of having, because they are not threatened by losing or not having. To the contrary, they are liturgies which make sense of our mini- and maxi-deaths and losses. They refresh the heart that has known surrender to death of some kind, such as the death of the illusion that we really have control over our lives. It is precisely the mystery of such surrender that the liturgies of having cannot comprehend. It is precisely the mystery of surrender which they abhor and shove aside, at first with indifference, but if pushed, then with violence. And the poor, the outcasts, the disenfranchised become fearful, terrible reminders to the celebrants of the liturgies of having that they are empty. From that marriage of illusion with fear is born many a demon that enslaves our world.

But when finally we allow the painful awareness of our poverty to BE, namely, that we can never "have" enough, then we can discover the joy of living with open hands. And true wealth will fill us all. "See, I make all things new."

But when finally we allow the lines of advancing age to BE just as they are, then we can discover the beautifully etched, unique character of each precious face. And true wisdom will blossom. "See, I make all things new."

But when finally we allow the silence of aloneness to be the breathing space between each word of intimacy, then we can discover that *ALL* of us are alone together. And true communion grows. "See, I make all things new."

When we are fully attuned to the elusive truth of surrender, then we can fully appreciate John's vision on Patmos. Telling the world what he sees there is what we Christian folk are about when we worship. We proclaim to a partly resistant and partly intrigued world that our blessedness is not in our having but in our being. We *are* poor. We *are* alone. We *are* aging and headed for the tomb. And, above all, we *are* loved. Justice is not likely to rule the earth until that awareness has fully claimed the human heart.

The cathedral in Paris still stands, and tourists still flock to see it. Their lives may or may not be affected by what they see. If the distance remains between them and the struggles of being human, which sends the heart to seek the presence of the Holy One, then there will be trouble aplenty. But if somehow they stay long enough to hear the stones speak, perhaps Notre Dame, the soul of Paris, will survive one more onslaught, and the stones will be anointed one more time with holiness. Perhaps it will be.

Contributors

ARCHBISHOP RAYMOND G. HUNTHAUSEN is deeply and personally involved in the many issues of our time and of the Church. Archbishop Hunthausen has been described by admirers as "the quintessential Vatican II bishop." During his 11-year administration as Shepherd of the Diocese of Seattle, he has been actively involved in issues concerning the nuclear arms race, pro-life concerns, Southeast Asia refugee resettlement, sanctuary for Central Americans, housing for the poor and elderly, women's roles in Church and society, and ministry to and advocacy of the rights of racial and sexual minorities. Archbishop Hunthausen has also spoken out consistently and forthrightly on the evils of abortion and euthanasia. With widespread recognition for his involvement in the nuclear arms issue, Archbishop Hunthausen has been the recipient of numerous awards. Among them are: the Dr. Bruno Kreisky Foundation for Service of Human Rights of Vienna, Austria (November 1984), the National Federation of Priests' Councils (April 1986), and Catholic Peace Ministry in Oregon (May 1986), which renamed their "Peacemaker of the Year" Award to "The Hunthausen Award for Peace." In his installation homily Archbishop Hunthausen said, "I would pray that we might truly be a loving people who recognize that if peace is to come into our world, it must begin first with us, a people who strive to be at peace with themselves, at peace with God, and at peace with one another . . . I pray for unity . . . as Christians, we should bring the witness of unity for all to see . . . we are one body with one Lord."

SISTER DIANNE BERGANT, C.S.A. is Professor of Old Testament studies at Catholic Theological Union in Chicago. In addition to teaching summer sessions at several colleges and universities in the United States, she has lectured in the Republic of South Africa and Trinidad, West Indies. She is currently editor of *The Bible Today* and is a member of the Lectionary Subcommittee for the Bishops' Committee on the Liturgy. Sister Dianne's numerous publications include collaborative work on *An Ancient Language Lectionary* (Readings for Years A, B & C). She has also written many articles and conducted workshops in the areas of Scripture, biblical spirituality, and feminism.

SISTER THEA BOWMAN, F.S.P.A. PH.D. is currently on the faculty of the Institute of Black Catholic Studies, Xavier University, New Orleans, and is a consultant for Intercultural Awareness for the Diocese of Jackson, Mississippi. Through song, dance, poetry, drama, and story she spreads the message that people are gifted, that Black is beautiful, and that cross-cultural collaboration enriches both education and living. Sister Thea makes more than 100 public appearances each year, giving lecture-recitals, short courses, workshops, and conference presentations.

REVEREND J. BRYAN HEHIR is presently Counselor for Social Policy, Department of Social Development and World Peace. United States Catholic Conference. He is also Senior Research Scholar for the Kennedy Institute of Ethics, Georgetown University, and Research Professor of Ethics and International Politics, School of Foreign Service, Georgetown University. Father Hehir is a former director of the Office of International Justice and Peace, United States Catholic Conference, and was a staff member to the National Conference of Catholic Bishops' Ad Hoc Committee on War and Peace. He is the recipient of numerous awards and honorary degrees and has written extensively on ethics, particularly in areas pertaining to international conflict, the nuclear arms debate, the arms race, and human rights.

REVEREND JAMES LOPRESTI, S.J., PH.D. is Executive Director of the North American Forum on the Catechumenate and directs the ReMembering Church (reconciliation) institutes for the Forum. He is a former co-director of the Loyola Pastoral Institute in New York City and former Associate Professor of Liturgical Theology, Seminary of the Immaculate Conception, Huntington, New York, and has taught at Loyola University of Chicago and Weston School of Theology. Father Lopresti's Ph.D. studies focused on the experience of conversion in the R.C.I.A. He has lectured and written widely on the initiation and reconciliation of Christians and is the author of *Penance: A Reform Proposal for the Rite.* A founding member of the North American Academy of Liturgy, Father Lopresti's articles on liturgy have appeared in *Worship, New Catholic World, Hosanna,* and *Christian Initiation Resources.*